THE NATURE LIBRARY

OCEAN LIFE

LES HOLLIDAY

CRESCENT BOOKS
NEW YORK

This 1991 edition published by Crescent Books,
distributed by Outlet Book Company, Inc.,
a Random House Company, 225 Park Avenue South,
New York, New York 10003.

Printed and bound in Hong Kong

ISBN 0-517-05151-6

8 7 6 5 4 3 2 1

Library of Congress Cataloging-in-Publication Data
Ocean Life
     p. cm – (Nature Library)
   Includes index.
   Summary: Describes the variety of animals which live in the oceans of the
world.
     ISBN 0-517-05151-6 : $6.99
   1. Marine biology – Juvenile literature.   (1. Marine animals)   I. Series.
QH91.16.028 1991   90-41154
574.92 – dc20   CIP
                                                                            AC

Credits
Edited and designed: Ideas into Print, Vera Rogers and Stuart Watkinson
Picture Editors: Annette Lerner, John Kaprielian
Photographs: Photo Researchers Inc., New York, and Les Holliday
Commissioning Editor: Andrew Preston
Production: Ruth Arthur, Sally Connolly, David Proffit, Andrew Whitelaw
Director of Production: Gerald Hughes
Director of Publishing: David Gibbon
Typesetting: SX Composing Ltd.
Color separations: Scantrans Pte. Ltd., Singapore

The Author
Les Holliday has had a passion for the ocean world since childhood
and has developed skills as an advanced SCUBA diver, underwater
photographer and marine biologist. He has participated in field
trips and marine expeditions to many parts of the world, leading
expeditions on a number of occasions to the Red Sea and to the
Caribbean. As well as writing books, Les is a leading contributor of
articles and photographs to a wide range of hobbyist magazines.

CONTENTS

Above: A common clownfish nestling among the tentacles of its host anemone. To other small fish, the stinging cells of the anemone would spell paralysis and death, but the clownfish enjoys a privileged protection. Just one example of creatures living in harmony in the world beneath the waves.

Left: A redtailed surgeonfish, one of many boldly marked fishes that live on the world's coral reefs. The name 'surgeon' arises from the sharp, scalpel-like spines near the base of the tail.

THE IMMENSITY OF THE WORLD'S OCEANS

From outer space, the most distinctive feature of our planet is its oceans. From this viewpoint, it is quite clear that we live on an azure blue sphere dappled here and there with brown and green landmasses. In fact, more than two-thirds of the world's surface is covered by the oceans. If it is difficult to comprehend an area of such staggering proportions, accounting for some 224 million square kilometres (139 million square miles), try to imagine the marine life such an area is capable of supporting and you soon realize how vast a living resource our oceans really are.

The world beneath the oceans is not of a uniform depth – there are mighty chasms and vast mountain ranges, some in their dimensions overshadowing similar features above the surface. Around the coastline of most landmasses is a shelf of land that may extend for hundreds of kilometres out beneath the surface. This is usually referred to as the continental shelf, and is the richest area for marine life. It reaches down to depths of 180-300m (600-1,000ft) and at its outer margin the seabed falls steeply into the abyss. The deepest point in the ocean floor is the Marianas Trench in the Pacific Ocean off the island of Guam, which is 10.5km(6.25 miles) below the surface.

Largely unexplored, the oceans still hold many secrets left to unravel. What we do know is that there is an immense variety of different habitats that marine life forms have exploited to the full. In many ways, their accomplishments have overshadowed those of man. A fitting example would be the Great Barrier Reef off the coast of Australia, which has been totally constructed by millions of tiny coral animals and represents the largest structure built by any life form.

Left: The cold oceans of the Arctic and Antarctic regions might appear at first sight to be inhospitable wastes of ice, devoid of life. However, the reverse is true, as the sea water around the poles abounds in nutrients and supports a rich and varied range of sea life. The whole of the Arctic consists of one huge ocean, because there is no Arctic continent, while the Antarctic Ocean surrounds the landmass at the South Pole. Man still has much to explore.

Above: The world viewed from the meteosat weather satellite, showing Africa, Europe, the Middle East and part of South America. It is clear to see that even these huge landmasses are dwarfed by the immensity of the oceans, which cover two-thirds of the earth's surface.

Above: The reefs of the Great Barrier Reef of Australia extend off the Queensland coast for over 2,300km (1,440 miles). They have been built up by millions of tiny coral animals.

Right: A close view of a colony of coral polyps, the tiny jellylike animals that create limestone cups around themselves and, in the process, build up huge coral reefs in warm tropical waters.

Right: Whales are familiar with the immensity of the oceans, because many undertake long migrations. Some species spend the summer in polar waters, where food is plentiful, and winter in the less hostile conditions of the warmer seas, where they breed and rear their young.

THE OCEANS – STOREHOUSE OF LIFE

All living things owe their origins to the simple forms of life that first appeared on our planet over 3,000 million years ago. These primitive life forms slowly evolved in the oceans as they became shaped mainly by their environment, and it was not until a mere 350 million years ago that the first living organisms invaded the land. By this time, the creatures of the oceans were well established and many would have been recognizable with their counterparts of today. Corals and sponges would be easily identifiable, together with molluscs, worms and other invertebrate forms. Sharks very similar to modern species roamed the oceans and prototype forms of the first bony fishes had begun to emerge.

There are many reasons why the sea was the birthplace of life and why it has continued to be a rich source of a wide variety of life forms. The sea is rich in nutrients and provides much more stable conditions than those on dry land. The dense salty water is also better able to support the bodies of living organisms, from tiny and fragile planktonic creatures to the massive bulk of the blue whale, the largest animal ever to have existed on earth. It is not surprising, therefore, that the lure of living on dry land was not able to prevent large groups of animals and plants 'choosing' to return to their former marine environment, notable among them the whales, dolphins and porpoises.

The wide diversity of life in the oceans today is to be found from the brightest shallows to the darkest depths and from warm lagoons around the equator to the chill waters that lap the polar ice caps. In all their diverse environments, the oceans provide a great profusion and variety of life and harbour some of the most beautiful and often bizarre creatures. Within the pages of this book we explore this fascinating world largely hidden beneath the surface of the sea.

Right: Sharks evolved 400 million years ago and so successful was their basic design that present-day sharks are almost identical to their early forebears in the primeval oceans.

Left: Many of the life forms that first evolved in the oceans millions of years ago still exist today. Sponges, such as this stunning purple tube variety photographed in the Caribbean Sea, appeared in the oceans at the very dawn of life, 1,000 million years ago. They continue to prosper in their original form, mainly because the conditions that prevailed then have remained unchanged and there has been no need for them to evolve further in the meantime.

Right: The oceans are so rich in nutrients that large numbers of animals can easily exist side by side, simply by staying in one place and feeding on the planktonic 'soup' passing by on the water currents. The success of this feeding technique is well illustrated here, with every available space taken up by plankton-feeding life forms, each one occupying its own small niche. Their diversity of shape allows them to take the best advantage of the habitat.

Left: The oceans are home to a great profusion and variety of life. These masses of big-eye fish feed primarily on the larger creatures of the animal plankton. They occur in large schools and are found mainly in the warmer regions of the Atlantic, north as far as Nova Scotia and south to Rio de Janeiro.

Below: Some examples of the various forms of phytoplankton, the microscopic plants of the sea. These live by absorbing chemicals from the water and using the sun's energy to convert these into food. They grow and multiply and become the food of zooplankton, which is eaten by many sea animals.

LIFE AT THE MARGINS OF THE SEA

Of all the marine environments, the shoreline is the most hostile. The animals and plants of temperate tidal seas must endure exposure to air at low tide, resulting in rapid dehydration, and the pounding of waves at high tide or when the sea is rough. Conditions along the margins of tropical oceans can be equally severe, but here there are two contrastingly different shoreline habits: the exposed beach and the cool shady conditions of the tidal mangrove forest.

Bathed in brilliant sunshine, the exposed sandy beach in tropical regions is a particularly harsh environment. At low tide, most of the animals retreat into holes or under rocks and boulders, and some burrow beneath the sand to avoid the blistering heat of the day. Plants have evolved tough, leathery leaves and long taproots to withstand drying out. A number of invertebrates, such as the ghost crab of the tropical Indian Ocean, build permanent burrows above high water mark and have almost become land creatures. Some hermit crabs have also forsaken their marine environment and spend their entire lives out of water.

By contrast, the mangrove forest provides a cool shady canopy and a rich habitat for a wide range of animals. The mangrove tree is a marvellous plant; it can grow in saline, waterlogged conditions and endures the fluctuations of high and low tides. It also acts as a 'larder' and a nursery area for many fishes and other creatures that thrive as adults on adjacent coral reefs. Silt becomes trapped beneath the

mangrove trees and combines with the rotting mangrove leaf litter to produce highly fertile conditions. Crabs, shelled molluscs and a whole range of other invertebrates abound in this nutrient-rich ooze. This squelchy terrain also forms the ideal habitat for one peculiar fish species, the mudskipper, which literally 'skips' across the damp mud.

Left: The silt and rotting material trapped around the roots of mangrove trees provide a fertile area that sustains a range of animals, such as shellfish and crabs, which revel in the ooze.

Below: A small colony of ascidians, or sea squirts, clings to a mangrove root. These simple jellylike animals live in association with mangroves and feed on plankton in the water.

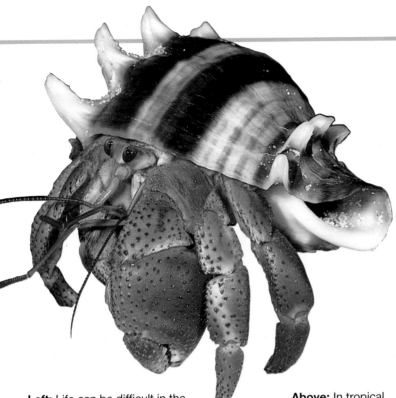

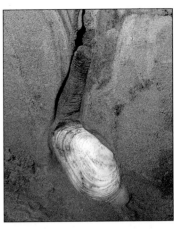

Right: One way of escaping dehydration and predation on the open beach is to bury deep in the sand. This geoduck clam excavates a tunnel with its foot and, once covered, breathes through its tubelike siphon.

Below: Ghost crabs are found in large numbers on tropical beaches all over the world. These dedicated and agile scavengers scurry along the beach, but always remain close to the refuge of their burrows.

Left: Life can be difficult in the hostile conditions of temperate tidal seas. As the tide recedes, it strands many animals above water and they must withstand rapid dehydration. The starfish, anemone and seaweed seen here are typical examples.

Above: In tropical regions of the world, many crabs spend their entire lives out of the water. The hermit crab shown here is one example, a common sight in southern Florida, lumbering along carrying its heavy shell.

Left: The shoreline, however hostile, provides a nesting ground for many seabirds. At breeding times, large noisy colonies of nesting birds, such as these gannets, often form.

Below: The straplike leaves of the leathery kelp can withstand drying out at low tide. Their holdfasts prevent heavy seas from dislodging them from their anchoring points on the rocks.

LIFE IN TROPICAL SEAS

Unlike the colder seas, the tropical oceans are not generally well provided with nutrients. This is because the salty, nutrient-laden water is relatively heavy and lies trapped beneath the less dense, warmer surface layers. There are also fewer areas where nutrients well up from the depths, as are found in temperate and polar seas. Nevertheless, tropical waters are often very productive in terms of marine life because of one very major asset – they bask beneath a canopy of blue skies and brilliant sunshine. Just like plants on land, plants in the sea can use the energy of the sun to bind basic chemicals together in the water to make food. This process of photosynthesis can be accomplished very efficiently in tropical sunshine and plants have evolved to cope with the low nutrient conditions.

Coral reefs are a major feature of tropical seas and are a marvellous example of how important sunshine can be. Reef-building corals can only succeed in well-lit shallow waters, in order that the tiny plant cells within their polyps – the zooxanthellae – can function. The success of reaping the 'sunshine harvest' is evident in the crowded environment of the reef, which is able to produce more animal and plant material for a given area than any other environment above or below the water.

The fuel used by this amazingly productive living factory consists mainly of chemicals and nutrients released from decaying plant material in adjacent lagoon and mangrove areas. These areas are also a rich source of plankton and are favoured nurseries for small fish fry and other young creatures. In turn, the plankton and fry become the food for many forms of life on the reef, activating the early stages of a complex food web.

Below: The coral reef is home to a wide variety of fish. More species live together on a coral reef than in any other undersea environment. Triggerfishes such as this are represented on most reefs.

Below: Because of competition for space and food, some reef fishes are nocturnal, hiding during the day and hunting for food after dark.

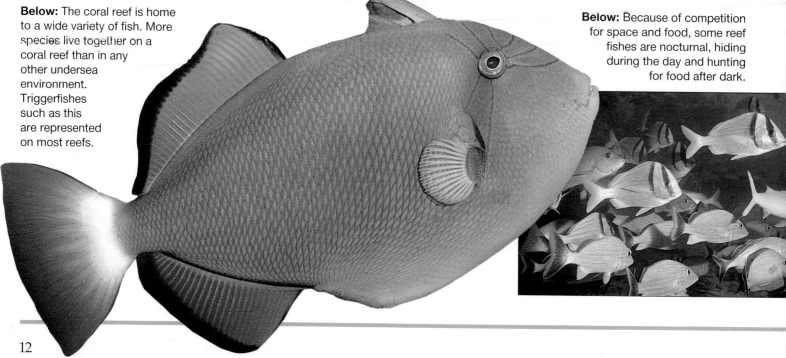

Below: The coral reef is a crowded environment and very productive in terms of its wide diversity of animals and plants.

Right: Tropical waters are the place to find the exotic and the bizarre. This nautilus is just such a creature – one of the last remaining species of shelled cephalopods. At one time, all squid, octopus and cuttlefish had external shells like this.

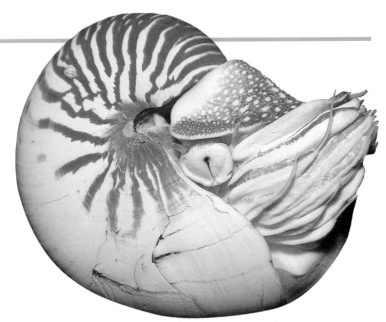

Below: Many reef animals have learned to live in harmony with one another. However, there are certain communal rules that must be obeyed. Many reef fishes are highly territorial and will fight to the death to protect their small individual territories.

Below: One unique tropical Atlantic undersea environment is formed by sargassum weed, which floats freely and is home to many peculiar animals.

Right: Angelfishes are some of the most beautiful reef fishes. With its gold and blue markings, this Caribbean queen angel is one of the most distinctive.

CORALS – ANIMALS OR PLANTS?

A major feature of tropical seas are the massive structures we call coral reefs. These are built up by an enormous variety of different life forms, often intermingled, to form one vast living community. The basic structure of the reef is composed of the skeletal remains of stony corals, tiny jellylike animals similar to sea anemones. Over thousand of years, succeeding generations of these coral polyps have deposited layer upon layer of hard limestone as a protective outer skeleton and in so doing have formed the coral reefs we see today. This is a never-ending process; the limestone laid down by the millions of polyps that have produced our present-day reef formations still continues to build up day by day.

Corals flourish in brightly lit, clean, warm water. Because of their colour and shape, it is not surprising that corals were once mistaken for plants. Indeed, some really do look like herbaceous plants while others become remarkably treelike in shape. From this point of view, the term 'coral gardens' seems very apt.

In ideal conditions, corals develop into three basic types of reef structure, depending on the depth of water and on the shape and movement of the seabed. Where the shore slopes steeply, the coral forms long growths parallel to the shore to produce a fringing reef. Classic examples of fringing reefs are found in the Red Sea and in parts of the Caribbean. In shallow seas, these fringing reefs may occur long distances offshore and form barrier reefs, such as the Great Barrier Reef off Australia, which is over 2,300km(1,440 miles) long and up to 200km(125 miles) wide in places. Where fringing reefs form around islets and the land subsides below sea level, circular or doughnut-shaped coral atolls develop. These are common in remote areas of the Pacific Ocean, forming classic 'desert islands'.

Above: An aerial view of the massive coral structures surrounding a South Pacific island. The island was formed by an active volcano and the corals grew up around its margins, producing a fringing reef.

Below: These colonial zoanthids, close relatives of the stony corals, share the jellylike structure and tentacles of those anemonellke creatures. They encrust rocks and sometimes other corals and sponges.

Left: The polyps of this stony coral colony are extending to feed, revealing tiny transparent tentacles. Fully extended, the polyps will eventually cover over their limestone cups.

Left: Not all corals live encased within calcereous skeletons. Some species, such as the beautiful, delicately branched *Dendronephthya* soft coral, are supported by an internal skeleton of limestone crystals known as sclerites.

Above: Some stony corals develop into large individual coral heads, known as coral massives. These huge natural formations provide shelter for many species of fish and other animals, and represent the main structure of the reef.

Left: Branching forms of soft corals are supported by a horny flexible material that is able to withstand the strong wave action that occurs in their natural habitat. They sway in the currents and have been given the popular name of sea whips.

Below: Although most corals flourish in brightly lit conditions, there are species that live in deeper, darker waters. These are the gorgonian corals, known as non-photosynthetic species because they do not need bright light to thrive.

THE DAZZLING WORLD OF CORAL REEF FISHES

Of all marine fishes, coral reef fishes are the most colourful. Their world is a bewildering confusion of gaudily patterned fish, overwhelming in numbers and diversity; in fact, there are more species of fish on the coral reef than in any other watery environment. We do not fully understand why there is such a wide diversity of fish species, but we do know that life forms evolve, or adapt, to their environment and in response to competition for space and food. Coral fishes no doubt evolved together with the reef-building corals, responding and adapting with them to produce the closely integrated ecosystem we see today.

Reef fishes can best be grouped according to their feeding patterns. Some feed on algae, spending the daylight hours browsing on the thin coating of algae that adheres to dead coral rock surfaces. Large numbers of shoaling species in brightly coloured clouds feed on tiny floating animals – the zooplankton, hovering on the reef edge where the richest concentrations occur. Some of the most beautiful reef fishes, including angelfishes and butterflyfishes, actually feed on coral polyps and sponges. Another important group, containing a large number of fish families such as snappers, puffers, triggers and some wrasses and emperors, feeds on other invertebrate life forms, such as molluscs, crustaceans and echinoderms. In the final group are the marine predators that feed mainly on other fish, and these include the sharks, groupers, moray eels and barracudas.

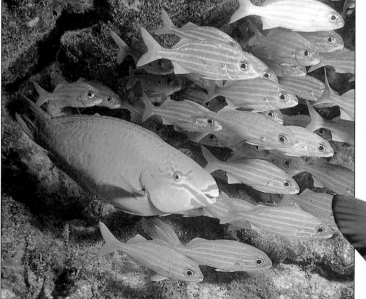

Left: The queen parrotfish is a daytime feeding herbivore that grazes on algae. It is shown here together with a group of small-mouthed grunts – carnivorous, nocturnal feeders.

Above: Colourful fairy basslets, or jewelfishes, are tiny cousins of the large predatory groupers. These lively fish, found in the Indian and Pacific Oceans, feed on upwelling zooplankton.

Left: Tiny bright green chromis live in small shoals close to spiky growths of staghorn corals, into which they retreat for safety. These fishes feed on zooplankton.

Above: Classifying reef fishes according to their feeding pattern is not so easy with opportunistic feeders, such as the surgeonfishes. This flagtail surgeonfish, or regal tang, feeds on filamentous algae. The name 'surgeon' comes from the sharp scalpels at the base of the tail.

Left: Groupers, such as this Panama graysby photographed off the Galapagos, are located at the top of the food chain, together with other large predators, including sharks, barracudas and moray eels. They are territorial animals that lie in wait for their prey, such as small fish and crustaceans.

Right: Triggerfishes are true opportunists, flitting across the reef searching for a quick meal. They feed on the most unlikely fare: the queen triggerfish illustrated here, specializes on long-spined *Diadema* sea urchins. This triggerfish from the tropical western Atlantic grows up to 50cm(20in) long.

Left: Angelfishes are common in shallow reef areas in all parts of the world. The adult Caribbean rock beauty shown here is very striking, with a dark area covering two-thirds of its vivid yellow body, but juveniles are yellow with just a small dark spot. Like many angelfishes, the rock beauty feeds on sponges.

INVERTEBRATES THAT FLOURISH ON THE CORAL REEF

The term 'invertebrate' simply means animals without a backbone. The largest proportion of all the animals on land or under the sea are invertebrates, and the total number of marine invertebrates is staggering, with possibly over a million species distributed worldwide in all the oceans. Coral reef invertebrates represent a major group, and one of the delights of a living reef is the wide range of colourful invertebrates that form a spectacular matrix of multihued corals interspersed with sponges, anemones and other decorative, brightly coloured creatures.

Looking first at the non-moving, or 'sessile' invertebrates, the coelenterates rank as the most important group. They include the reef-building corals, sea fans and anemones, together with the more mobile jellyfishes. Sponges often accompany the corals, and can make up a large proportion of the reef structure, especially in the Caribbean. The final significant 'stay put' group are the fanworms, beautiful featherduster-like creatures that disappear instantly into their tubes when approached.

The most conspicuous and mobile invertebrates are the crustaceans, sometimes called the 'insects of the sea'. They include crabs, lobsters and shrimps. The slower-moving molluscs are represented on the reef by the shellfish and sea slugs, but also include the more active squid, cuttlefish and octopi. The final major group of mobile invertebrates are the entirely marine animals that belong to the echinoderms. They are typified on coral reefs by starfishes and sea urchins, but sea cucumbers, featherstars and sea lilies are also prominent members of this group.

Above: Reef-building corals, such as these elkhorn corals, are made up of millions of tiny living coral polyps. These are constantly in the process of growing and multiplying to produce the limestone structures that we call reefs. There are many forms of reef-building corals, and a well-formed reef can provide a spectacular array of shapes.

Left: Crustaceans are like aquatic insects and are described as invertebrates because in place of an internal backbone they have a hard external skeleton. This candy shrimp is a good example.

Right: Seafans appear to be more like plants than animals. They are another form of coral and are covered in thousands of tiny polyps, which trap and devour microscopic planktonic animals. This one comes from the Caribbean, where seafans are common on the reefs.

Left: Sponges are very varied in colour and shape, and as many as nine separate species are vividly displayed here. Their ability to regenerate and adapt have ensured their survival. They are a prominent feature of reefs all over the world, but are most abundant in the Caribbean, where there are whole reefs consisting mainly of sponges.

Above: The echinoderms are a major invertebrate group found on coral reefs. Starfishes, with their five or more arms, are familiar members of this group.

Below: The *Tridacna* clam, in common with many stony corals, plays host to algae in its tissues. They are clearly visible here in the fleshy blue mantle.

Below: Surprisingly, the slow-moving sea slug, or nudibranch, is a carnivore that devours a variety of other invertebrates. This attractive species was photographed off Papua New Guinea.

Above: Crinoids are a kind of feathery starfish. They have evolved to become nocturnal filter-feeders and trap microscopic zooplankton in their feathery arms. They remain hidden during the day.

LIFE IN TEMPERATE WATERS

The temperate seas are richly populated with life forms that have adapted to the hostile conditions of their environment. The low temperatures, often violent weather and large tidal differences that are a feature of temperate waters are harsh on sea life. If animals and plants are to survive, they must be able to withstand the full force of breaking waves in the shallows and dehydration when stranded at low tide. The cold winters of temperate climes can be equally damaging. In the North Atlantic, for example, drastic seasonal temperature changes can inflict severe winter losses on marine animals, and each spring, stocks of sea urchins, starfishes and molluscs are replenished by juveniles born the previous season that migrated into deeper waters for the winter. On the other hand, the plants and animals of the North Pacific are not subject to such harsh winter conditions. Invertebrate life on the Californian coast north to British Columbia is more extensive and varied than in the North Atlantic, because the creatures have a longer lifespan and can survive from one year to the next.

There are two principal undersea environments in temperate waters: rocky seabed and sand. The hard, rocky bottom provides the best conditions and here seaweeds have evolved with 'holdfasts' in place of roots that ensure a secure grip on the hard surfaces. The leaves of these plants are often leathery, flat and straplike to withstand the rough conditions. Some

animals, such as limpets, sea anemones and sea snails, attach themselves to the rocks by means of strong suckers. There are far fewer plants on sandy seabeds and, consequently, a smaller number of animals. Lacking the cover and shelter provided by plants, only those animals capable of burrowing into the sand can feed and survive. These include burrowing fishes, crabs, shrimps and sea urchins, as well as a variety of molluscs and worms.

Left: The main harvest from the sea is fish. Man takes more than 55 million tonnes (more than 120 billion pounds) of fish from the sea each year. The bulk of this comes from temperate waters.

Below: Tough leathery leaves and a strong holdfast are not always sufficient protection in harsh temperate waters. These kelp fronds have become detached and washed ashore.

Left: The richly populated waters of temperate climes provide a bounty of food for those creatures that can tolerate the hostile conditions. Violent weather and large tidal changes mean that only the hardiest are able to survive here.

Right. You could easily be forgiven for believing that the brilliant orange Californian Garibaldi fish belongs on a coral reef. Such vivid coloration is unusual in temperate waters, where drab colours are the usual order of the day.

Below: These limpets are clinging tenaciously to the base of an intertidal boulder. A strong sucker disc attaches these tough molluscs firmly to the rock surface and a protective shell prevents them dehydrating when the tide goes out.

Above: The animals found in British Columbian waters have a longer lifespan than their counterparts in the North Atlantic. Because the winters are warmer, starfishes, such as this northern sunstar, are able to survive and grow very large.

Left: The North Atlantic winter flounder chooses to live in a sandy environment. It has a highly compressed body and the amazing ability to change its body coloration and markings to match its surroundings perfectly. Both eyes are located on the top surface of the adult fish.

FISHES THAT LIVE IN TEMPERATE SEAS

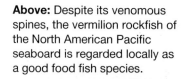

Fishes from temperate waters tend to be less colourful than those from the tropics, and there are fewer species. However, there are many more individuals of each species, quite simply because the abundance of food in temperate waters allows more individuals, all eating the same food, to survive. Many species shoal in large numbers and are, therefore, easy to catch. Herring, cod and haddock and their relatives, for example, have considerable commercial value, and flatfishes, such as plaice and sole, are also important foods.

Flatfishes have evolved to become perfectly adapted to life in sandy conditions. When they hatch, flatfish fry look just like other fish and are free swimming. However, as they develop, their eyes gradually move to one side as the body becomes flattened. This body shape, combined with the ability to change colour and markings to match their surroundings, is ideally suited to life in the flat sandy bottom, where the fish often bury themselves until only their eyes are visible.

The large, predatory carnivorous fish include some fascinating and unusual species. The John Dory, for example, is a curious fish, with a flattened plate-shaped body, massive head and permanently mournful expression. This toothless predator stalks small fish, extending its mouth to seize its prey in one rapid engulfing action. The most formidable species, however, is perhaps the wolf fish, found in North Atlantic waters. It grows over 1m(39in) long and its size, combined with the wolflike head and rows of protruding teeth capable of crushing the shells of the adult crabs on which it feeds, give it a nightmarish quality.

Above: Despite its venomous spines, the vermilion rockfish of the North American Pacific seaboard is regarded locally as a good food fish species.

Below: Ocean sunfishes are summer visitors to temperate waters. These plankton feeders can grow up to 3m(10ft) long and weigh a tonne(2,200lb).

Below: Commercially fished North Atlantic species include the whiting, shown here, and its close relations the haddock and the cod. These and other fish play an important role in the economy of many countries.

Right: Perfectly adapted to survive in sandy seabed conditions, the turbot often lies buried beneath the sand, revealing only its eyes. This is a highly effective defence against a variety of predators.

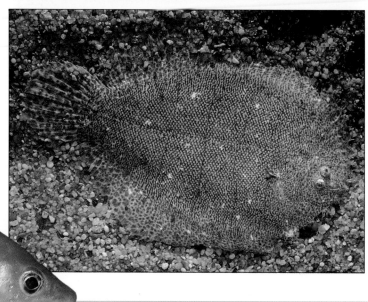

Above: The general observation that fishes from temperate waters are less colourful than those from the tropics does not apply to the red Irish lord found in the cold waters off British Colombia in northern Canada. Out of the water, this fish is as striking as any of its tropical cousins, but remember that in underwater conditions, red appears as a drab grey.

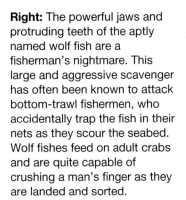

Left: The John Dory is a wily and very successful hunter, but it is not built to chase its prey. Instead, it lies in wait or slowly stalks the small fish that it favours, its narrow body almost invisible when viewed head-on. Its jaws have evolved in such a way that they are able to shoot forward in a lightning strike to engulf its unsuspecting meal.

Above: The cod is, perhaps, the most important of the commercial fish species found in temperate waters. It is widely distributed in the northern Atlantic, from the North Sea to Labrador, and extends into the icy Arctic waters off Greenland, Iceland and Newfoundland. In recent years, fishing has been controlled to conserve stocks.

Right: The powerful jaws and protruding teeth of the aptly named wolf fish are a fisherman's nightmare. This large and aggressive scavenger has often been known to attack bottom-trawl fishermen, who accidentally trap the fish in their nets as they scour the seabed. Wolf fishes feed on adult crabs and are quite capable of crushing a man's finger as they are landed and sorted.

INVERTEBRATE LIFE IN TEMPERATE SEAS

The cool waters of the North Atlantic are hardly the place you would expect to find coral reefs, but there are corals that grow and thrive in temperate waters. They are not the same as the stony corals that build reefs in the tropics, but alcyonarian soft corals. The common species found in European waters has earned itself the descriptive name of 'dead man's fingers'. Furthermore, these pretty, delicate corals are not the only exotic-looking coelenterates. There are also many colourful sea anemones that would not look out of place in the tropics. However, temperate water invertebrates are generally drab in colour and camouflaged to match their surroundings.

Plant-eating herbivorous invertebrates are a common sight among the rich forests of kelp and other seaweeds on which they feed. Many shellfishes fall into this category, such as abalone in North Pacific waters, and limpets, winkles and other forms of sea snails in the North Atlantic. Sea urchins are another important herbivore group. The starfishes, close relations of the sea urchins, are, by contrast, rather unlikely-looking carnivorous hunters, moving slowly on tiny tube feet across the seabed. Nevertheless, they are successful predators of a wide range of animals and especially fond of bivalve molluscs, such as mussels and oysters. They attack them by prising open the two shells of the animal and applying a firm, constant pressure until the poor mollusc finally gives way from sheer exhaustion. The role of scavenger falls to the crabs, lobsters and shrimps, all of which are well represented in temperate waters.

Right: Starfishes are a common feature of temperate waters. One amazing ability of these creatures is their powers of regeneration. Severed arms, for example, quickly grow back.

Right: Carnivorous sea slugs such as this feed on a range of invertebrates.

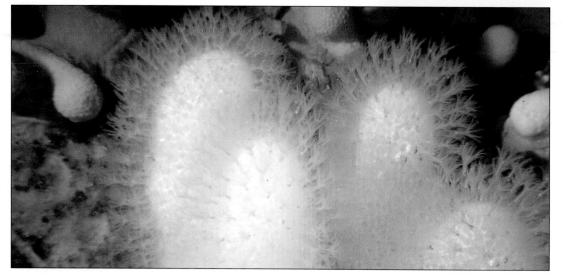

Above: This North Atlantic edible sea urchin has feeler tentacles, which are modified tubelike feet. Each tube foot has a tiny sucker that enables the urchin to get a grip and haul itself about. Sea urchins and starfishes are closely related.

Left: Feathery white alcyonarian soft corals create an exotic, almost tropical appearance on the rocky seabeds of their temperate waters habitat. The common name of 'dead man's fingers' perfectly describes their bleached fingerlike proportions, which have scared many a diver.

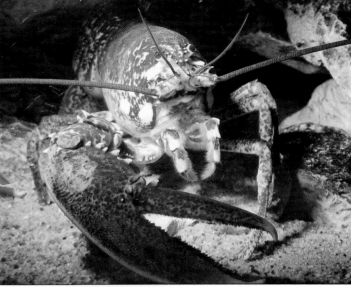

Above: The large-clawed lobster is restricted to temperate waters. It is a major commercial species, fished in the open seas and also raised on fish farms. The pincerlike claws are dangerous at close quarters, easily able to crush a finger.

Left: This beautiful anemone is only one of a large number of very colourful species, widely distributed in all the temperate seas. These carnivorous marine animals use their tentacles to sting prey and pass the victim into the central mouth opening.

Below: Many invertebrates from temperate waters are good for eating, and the edible crab shown here is no exception. Caught in large numbers for the table, this opportunistic feeder is found in many areas of the Atlantic and Pacific Oceans.

THE POLAR SEAS – COLD BUT PRODUCTIVE

The waters of the polar seas are both very cold and very salty. The reason for the high degree of salinity can be traced to the extensive icefields and icebergs. These huge masses of ice consist of almost totally pure water, the salts having been left behind during the freezing process. The salts that accumulate in the remaining unfrozen water encourage the growth of phytoplankton, the only plant life found in polar regions. It is especially abundant during the summer months, when the sunlight is at its strongest. In the complex food web, tiny planktonic shrimps (generally called 'krill') feed on the abundant phytoplankton, multiply in huge numbers and, in turn, become food for a wide range of zooplankton-feeding animals, from anemones and soft corals up to the mighty blue whale, which is found in large numbers feeding in polar regions during the summer.

The polar seas are not, therefore, the lifeless frozen waters you might imagine, but support quite a diversity and abundance of marine animals. In the Northern Hemisphere, the polar seas are home to enormous shoals of fishes and provide major fishing grounds for herring, cod and blue whiting. Even the seabed below the ice cap at the North Pole is surprisingly well populated with various forms of invertebrate life, including swarms of tiny crustaceans, starfishes, soft corals and anemones. A number of totally aquatic mammals live permanently in the polar

regions, including seals, walruses and killer whales. During the summer, they are joined by migrant populations of baleen whales. The polar regions of the Southern Hemisphere also abound with life. Penguins are the birds we associate with the frozen wastes, and all 17 species are confined to the Southern Hemisphere.

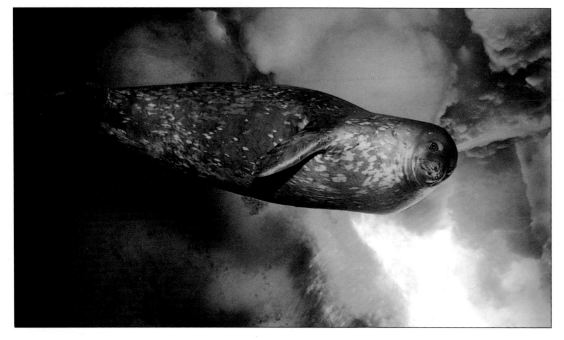

Above: The huge expanses of pack ice and icebergs that are a common feature of both polar regions of the world are responsible for the high degree of salinity in these waters. This icy cold terrain above the water also provides a habitat for a wide range of aquatic mammals and birds. They rest here between excursions above and below the water surface.

Left: Marine aquatic animals, such as this Weddell seal, are perfectly at home in polar regions, their bodies protected by thick layers of fat, popularly called 'blubber'. Although air breathing, seals can make quite long excursions below the ice in search of prey – mainly fish.

Above: The aptly named chinstrap penguin is a common Antarctic species. Each year it raises one or two chicks during the short Antarctic summer. These normally inoffensive birds will fight to protect their young.

Below: The humpback whale is one of the large baleen whales that migrate to polar regions each summer to feed on tiny crustaceans called 'krill'. They use their long baleen plates to filter the krill from the water.

Above: Beneath the water, penguins move with skill and grace.

Above: Animals that feed on the abundant zooplankton take many forms. This huge Antarctic jellyfish is a major carnivore in these icy waters, disabling small fish and shrimps with the batteries of vicious stinging cells that cover its trailing, almost invisible tentacles.

THE DIVERSITY OF SEA MAMMALS

Sea mammals fall into two groups, those that live permanently in the sea and never, or perhaps only occasionally, visit dry land, and those that live on land but hunt for food in the sea. The first group are outstanding in the variety of ways they have adapted to a totally aquatic environment and often extremely difficult living conditions. For example, certain mammals have adapted to thrive in the chill conditions of the polar seas.

Whales and dolphins must rank as the best examples of mammals totally adapted to an aquatic life, unable to live on land, but feeding, sleeping and reproducing in the water. Like the whales and dolphins, seals and sea cows have retained limited use of their forelimbs, but their hind limbs have fused together to form a paddlelike tail or flippers. Seals can clamber out of the water, but are very vulnerable because their limbs and body movement are so poorly adapted to life on dry land. In water, on the other hand, they have no difficulty, being athletic swimmers, easily able to hunt down their prey of fish. The related sea lions and walruses can swivel their hind flippers forward and are thus less cumbersome on land. Sea cows - dugongs and manatees – are totally aquatic herbivores, feeding on sea grasses. These gentle creatures, related to elephants, are confined to the warm Indian Ocean and tropical Atlantic, and are usually found in coastal lagoons and river estuaries.

Sea otters are identical to land otters, but live in kelp beds off the Pacific coast of California. At one time, they were hunted for their fur and came close to extinction, but steps are now being taken to conserve

the species. In fact, the plight of the sea otter brought the interdependence of marine life sharply into focus. Without a predator, its prey – mainly sea urchins – increased in numbers and threatened the kelp beds by feeding on the holdfasts of the plants. The depletion of the kelp in turn reduced the numbers of abalone, a mollusc living in the kelp beds. Thankfully, conservation of the sea otter has reversed this process and restored the natural balance.

Above: By whale standards, the beluga is tiny, but it clearly demonstrates the link between whales and dolphins, with its dolphinlike appearance and antics. Totally adapted to an aquatic life, the beluga, or white whale, grows only a little larger than its dolphin cousins.

Left: The sea otter is one of the few animals that has become adapted to using tools. Floating on its back on the water surface, the sea otter uses a large flat stone as an anvil on which it cracks open its shellfish prey by hammering it on the stone. Here, an otter is enjoying a clam, one of the species on which it feeds.

Left: Dolphins are a remarkable example of a mammal totally adapted to an aquatic life. So well adapted are these creatures to their watery environment that they often have time to relax from hunting for food and cavort playfully in the waves.

Right: The inoffensive manatee, one of the sea cows, browses on the rich pastures of aquatic vegetation. It is equally at home in fresh or sea water. Unfortunately, these huge gentle herbivores have been hunted almost to the point of extinction.

Below: The walrus is confined to the Arctic polar regions. It has developed long tusks to dig in the seabed for shellfish. With their curved shape, these tusks are ideally suited for raking through the gravel and pebbles.

Above: Sea lions and seals are athletic swimmers, easily able to hunt down and catch their prey of squid and small fishes. Their sharp pointed teeth are ideal for gripping their slippery meals.

Left: This harp seal, resting off the Gulf of St. Lawrence, shows how poorly adapted seals have become to life out of the water. Their ungainliness on land is in direct contrast to their agility and speed in the water.

WARM-BLOODED GIANTS OF THE OCEAN

Whales are warm-blooded, air-breathing mammals that bear live young and suckle them with milk. They are the largest animals in the world; the blue whale can reach 31m(almost 102ft) long; indeed, it is the largest creature ever to have lived, exceeding the largest of the prehistoric dinosaurs in size.

Whales fall into one of two major categories: the toothed whales and the baleen ('whalebone') whales. Toothed whales are carnivorous hunters with powerful jaws and sharp teeth. They range from the 8m(26ft)-long killer whale, which feeds on a wide range of animals, including seals, seabirds, fish and squid, and sometimes gathers in packs to attack and feed on other whales, to the sperm whale, which may grow up to 20m(65.5ft) long and feeds deep in the abyss, mainly on squid and octopi. Baleen whales, on the other hand, have huge comblike sieves made of keratin (the same substance as fingernails in man). These hang down from the roof of the mouth and the whale feeds by straining zooplankton and, in some whales, shoaling fish from the water through the baleen. There may be up to 400 of these plates on each side of the mouth in some baleen whales. The blue whale is a baleen whale, as are the right whales and the fin, sei, Bryde's, minke, humpback, bowhead and gray whales.

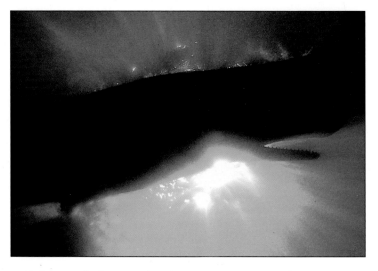

Baleen whales tend to be migratory, living in the cold waters of the polar seas in summer and migrating towards the equator in winter to breed and rear their young. Commercial whaling first started in the breeding grounds of these whales but, as they became scarce, first the Arctic and then the Antarctic became major hunting grounds. The persistent hunting of these gentle giants and the failure of international agencies to implement effective conservation measures means that some species are threatened with extinction.

Above: The sperm whale is the largest of the toothed whales, a formidable creature and the subject of countless stories from the early days of whaling, when it was hunted for its oil and spermaceti wax. It preys on squid and octopi. Many bear the scars of these encounters, and the remains of huge squid have been found in the stomachs of captured animals.

Left: The smallest of the toothed whales – the orca, or killer whale – is no less formidable than its larger relations, and renowned for its attacks on seals, baleen whales and on a wide range of other animals, even birds. Recent studies indicate that killer whales are very social creatures that live in small family groups, communicating with and caring for each other.

Left: The impressive sight of a humpback whale breaching. Note the long flippers.

Left: Swarming crustaceans called 'krill' provide a major part of the diet of baleen whales and are the food of the largest living animal, the blue whale.

Right: Humpback whales often feed in groups, encircling shoals of krill or small fish and then rising to the surface to engulf their prey, filtering the food in their sievelike baleen plates.

Left: A huge blue whale prepares to dive into the depths of the ocean, revealing a massive tail. At up to 31m (almost 102ft) long, this is the largest creature that has ever lived on earth and dwarfs the largest of the dinosaurs.

Below: The right whale earned its common name because it was said to be the 'right' whale to hunt, not only for its rich reserves of oil, but also because it remained afloat when killed. Clearly visible here are the horny growths called 'callosities'.

CLOWNS OF THE SEA

Dolphins and porpoises are close relatives of the whales. In fact, they are simply smaller members of the toothed whales. The simplest distinction between dolphins and porpoises is that dolphins usually have a distinct beak while porpoises have a blunt snout. Dolphins are perhaps the most familiar sea mammals, because many people have seen them in dolphinariums. These intelligent creatures seem to have a special association with man and there are many examples of wild dolphins approaching swimmers and acting in a friendly manner. Of course, this may simply be an expression of their social nature and caring instincts.

With the exception of a few river species, all dolphins and porpoises are marine, living mainly in temperate and tropical waters. They are carnivorous, feeding principally on fish, and are adept hunters. These playful animals often travel in schools, or herds, engaging in elaborate 'team games' with one another and leaping athletically out of the water.

In recent years, a great deal of study has concentrated on their amazing navigational sonar system. By emitting a series of high-pitched 'clicks', they are able to build up a 'sound picture' of their surroundings by interpreting the echoes they receive. In this way, dolphins and porpoises can find incredibly tiny objects in completely turbid water conditions and easily avoid obstructions while swimming at breakneck speeds.

Below: Communication between dolphins and humans is not solely a modern-day experience. There are records of similar encounters with these friendly animals reaching back many thousands of years.

Above: In its own environment, the open sea, this lone spotted dolphin in Hawaiian waters is a noble creature. This social animal is more commonly found in schools of up to several hundred animals.

Left: The popular conception of the dolphin is of a friendly creature, eager to entertain at the dolphinarium. The bottle-nose dolphin, shown here, is the most commonly kept in captivity. It is playful, intelligent and easily trained, and its amiable features have endeared it to spectators worldwide.

Below: The exuberance of this dusky dolphin as it leaps clear of the water illustrates the playful nature of these animals and their sheer joy of living. The dusky dolphin is one of the most sociable and acrobatic species.

Bottlenose dolphins need little incentive to perform – on the contrary, they positively seem to enjoy doing so. However, they eagerly accept their keeper's reward of a small fish. Dolphins can prove very innovative, often adding tricks of their own to the performance.

Left: Young dolphins appear to enjoy riding the bow waves of passing ships, being pushed along on the wave, leaping out of the water and racing forward to gain on the ship in order to repeat the process.

Below: This large school of spotted dolphins is indulging in a playful game of tag. There is often a definite structure to these play periods, with what appears to be elaborate rules of conduct. School sizes vary.

SEALS AND WALRUSES

Seals and walruses are some of the most widely distributed of all the mammals, occurring from the icy wastes of the poles to the Galapagos Islands on the equator. However, their natural habitat is usually among temperate and cold waters and it is only cold currents that have encouraged the seals to colonize the waters of the equatorial Galapagos Islands. Although all seals are much more at home in the water, they are not totally aquatic in the same way as whales, sea cows and sea otters, for example, because they need to go ashore to breed.

There are 34 species of seals and their allies, divided into three families – the eared seals (with small ear appendages), the true seals (without any detectable external ears), and the walruses (also without ears). The main feature that separates these groups are the flippers. In true seals, the hind flippers point permanently backwards, whereas eared seals and walruses can turn their hind flippers forward, dramatically improving their ability to move on land. The grey (or Atlantic) seal, elephant seal, leopard seal and common (or harbour) seal are all true seals, whereas the sea lions are eared seals.

Most seals feed on fish, squid and octopi and have sharp pointed teeth to grip their prey. The ferocious leopard seal of the Antarctic also attacks and feeds on penguins. Hunting alone, the leopard seal lurks near the water's surface beneath the overhang of an ice floe and shoots out to catch any unwary penguin that dives into the water. Walruses, which are only found in Arctic waters, sport two long tusks that they use to dig molluscs out of the seabed.

Above: The common, or harbour, seal is one of the so-called true seals. As shown here, these do not have detectable external ears.

Right: This huge bull sea lion is three times larger than the female. During the breeding season, bulls defend extensive territories and maintain harems often numbering 20 or more females.

Below: Every year, sea lions congregate in large colonies to breed on the Valdés Peninsula, Patagonia. These pups are only two weeks old, but already display the herding instinct of their parents. Adults and juveniles separate into groups.

Above: The harp seal of the Gulf of St. Lawrence is another member of the family of true seals and common over a wide area of the North Atlantic.

Right: The walrus is a large sea mammal; males may weigh over a tonne (2,200lb). This survivor of many battles is covered in puncture wound scars.

Below: During the breeding season, walruses herd together on the rocky beaches of the Bering Sea. Aggregations of over 3,000 have been recorded.

MARINE TURTLES – LONG-LIVED REPTILES OF THE SEA

Unlike mammals, reptiles are not able to control their body temperature by generating heat internally. Instead, they rely on the heat of the sun to 'energize' their bodily functions and, not surprisingly, most reptiles are, therefore, found in warm climates. Those that do live in temperate regions hibernate during the winter. Marine turtles are reptiles and no exception to this general rule, being distributed mainly in the tropical areas of the world.

There are two families of marine turtles: the leatherback is the single member of one of these families, while the remaining family includes the green turtle, the hawksbill, two species of loggerhead and two species of Ridley's turtle. A popular misconception is that all turtles feed on turtle grass, but only the green turtle is mainly herbivorous. Loggerheads and the Ridley turtles are mainly carnivorous, feeding on fish, crabs and shellfish, while the leatherback and hawksbill species take a wide range of animal and plant food.

In common with other reptiles, turtles are air-breathing, and cannot be considered totally aquatic, as they return to land to lay their eggs. When the female is ready to lay, she clambers ashore at night onto a selected deserted beach and ponderously makes her way above high water mark. Many turtles become lost or stranded during this journey, some becoming

wedged between tree roots and dehydrating in the hot sun the following day. Those that survive, bury their eggs in the sand. Even at this point, however, hazards remain because the process can exhaust the female to the point where she has insufficient strength to make the return journey to the sea.

During the incubation period, the buried eggs are constantly vulnerable to predators, but perhaps the most dangerous stage of the turtle's life is when the hatchlings make for the sea en masse. This usually signals a feast for their predators, and the baby turtles are attacked by seabirds, crabs and other animals as they run the gauntlet to the safety of the ocean.

Above: The Atlantic Ridley's turtle regularly visits the Gulf of Mexico and the Caribbean, coming ashore on the Central American coastline to lay its eggs, but otherwise remaining in the water. The Mexican government has recently taken steps to prevent the overfishing that is endangering this and other turtle species in the Gulf.

Left: The mighty loggerhead turtle has a worldwide distribution in tropical waters. This turtle takes at least 10 years to reach sexual maturity and a further 10 years to reach maximum size. Turtles can live much longer than this, however, and may have a greater lifespan than man. They can survive nearly 40 years in captivity.

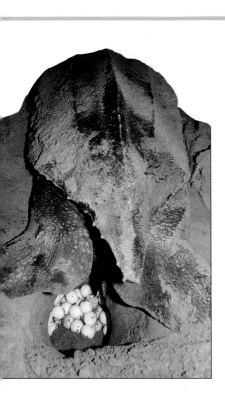

Above: Following a long and laborious clamber up the beach, this leatherback turtle excavates a hole in the sand and then proceeds to lay her eggs.

Above: The young Atlantic green turtle is an agile and proficient swimmer. This is one of the few herbivorous species, grazing on aquatic vegetation.

Below: The incubating eggs of the Ridley's turtle are shown here being preyed upon by vultures on a desolate beach in Puerto Rico. Even though the eggs are buried in the sand, they remain vulnerable to predation.

Above: On their way from the nest to the sea, these baby turtles seem to know they are in danger. After breaking cover from the nest, there follows a frantic dash to the sea to avoid the host of seabirds, crabs and other beach predators. Man has also been responsible for the decline in turtle numbers by overcollecting the eggs.

Right: Considering all the dangers that they face, it is surprising that any baby turtles manage to survive. This story does have a happy ending; a small group of loggerhead turtle hatchlings have successfully run the gauntlet of beach predators and reached the ocean. In this watery environment, the young have a better chance of survival.

VENOMOUS SEA SERPENTS

Marine snakes are another group of reptiles that have found their way back to the sea. There is a surprisingly large number of species, all confined to the Indian Ocean and adjacent areas of the Pacific Ocean near Australia. The Great Barrier Reef in Australia is home to over 30 species, all equipped with potent venomous fangs. Although sea snakes are not usually aggressive, the olive sea snake has been known to attack divers and swimmers and is perhaps the most lethal species.

Two main features distinguish sea snakes from land species. One is a flattened, paddle-shaped tail for making eel-like swimming movements, and the second is the small head and upper body that allow the snakes to dig easily into the sand for their usual prey of sand eels and small fish. In common with other reptiles, sea snakes are air-breathing, but are able to spend an hour or more submerged before they need to surface to replenish their air supply.

Sea kraits, found in the Pacific islands and Southeast Asia, return to the land to lay their eggs. However, the majority of species are livebearing, producing between two and ten live young at sea. There have been reports of breeding swarms of sea snakes, often of many thousands, appearing at certain times of the year.

Above: The reputation of the sea snake as a lethal aggressive animal is, perhaps, not well founded, as most species tend to avoid confrontation. However, divers would be well advised to take great care when handling such venomous animals.

Below: Banded sea snakes are a docile species, with poorly developed fangs and venom glands. They are widely distributed over the Indian and Pacific Oceans. This species belongs to the group that produce live young at sea.

Right: All sea snakes are carnivorous, feeding on a wide range of fish or their eggs. Some species hunt small fish, using their venomous fangs to disable them. Other species feed exclusively on fish eggs, and some burrow deep down into the sandy seabed in order to catch burrowing sand eels. The sea snake uses its keen sense of smell/taste to locate prey.

Below: Sea snakes are particularly well represented and common in the waters of the Philippines. Fishermen and divers need to take great care when reaching into holes and crevices in the reef, in order to avoid the chance of disturbing a resting sea snake. Some species have adopted warning coloration, whereas others are camouflaged for protection.

Above: The sea snake is an air-breathing animal that must regularly return to the water surface. However, most species can remain submerged for an hour or more. They are mainly found in shallow waters.

Below: Of all the sea snakes, the olive sea snake is regarded as the most dangerous. Unlike other species, it has a reputation for approaching divers and attacking ferociously. Thankfully, few attacks end with a bite.

SEA DRAGONS OF THE GALAPAGOS ISLANDS

The entire range of land animals living on the Galapagos Islands is believed to have arrived on these isolated specks of land as chance visitors from mainland South America, borne there as unwitting passengers on rafts of vegetation and other debris washed down into the rivers and out to sea. The volcanic Galapagos Islands are generally inhospitable to most forms of life, with a bleak vegetation consisting mainly of arid scrubland and cactus. Some of the iguanas washed onto these shores adapted to feeding on seaweed and evolved into the marine iguanas found there today. In fact, the Galapagos marine iguana is the only lizard that relies on the sea for its survival and only visits its marine environment to feed.

Being a reptile and thus not able to generate body heat internally, the Galapagos marine iguana is faced with something of a problem; although temperatures on these equatorial islands can be scorching, the sea is often chilly because the Humboldt Current draws cold water from the southern oceans and carries it northwards along the coasts of Chile and Peru. Life for the marine iguana, therefore, is made up of brief excursions into the cold ocean to feed, followed by long periods basking in the sun to regain its body heat. This lifestyle has forced the iguana to evolve elaborate means of displaying its body to the sun's rays in order to control its temperature adequately. For example, spread-eagling the body broadside to the sun allows for rapid warming, while facing the sun head-on reduces the body area exposed. By midday, even these manoeuvres are not sufficient and the iguanas crowd together in the sparse shade to cool down.

Left: Many species of land iguana construct burrows, and the Galapagos marine iguana is no exception to this general rule. Also in common with the land species, they bury their eggs in the sand so that they can be incubated by the sun's heat.

Right: When the sun is at its highest and hottest at midday, the marine iguanas of the Galapagos Islands crowd into any available shade to keep cool. Often, there is competition for the best positions, which causes overcrowding.

Left: Marine iguanas only enter the sea to feed on growths of seaweed in shallow water. They swim by rapidly beating their paddlelike tails and can descend to depths of 10m(30ft) or more.

Above: Foraging excursions into the cold sea can seriously lower the marine iguana's body temperature. Back on land, they bask in the sun, exposing as much of the body as possible.

Left: A Galapagos iguana stands its ground, knowing it has no natural predators. If disturbed, it will shoot a stream of salty water from its nostrils.

Right: The limited range of life forms on the Galapagos Islands means that there are fewer predators, and animals that would normally be under threat are able to move about freely in the open. Here, bright scarlet crabs mingle openly with the iguanas that are warming up in the sun following a morning's feeding in the cold seas.

Left: The male marine iguana is larger than the female and its dorsal crest is far more pronounced. The crest is displayed to the female during courtship and is used in aggressive displays towards other males during territorial disputes. Males often change colour during the breeding season, taking on red and orange hues.

BLENDING INTO THE BACKGROUND

The coral reef is an ideal place to study evolution, because so many of the animals in this crowded environment have evolved different survival strategies. Camouflage is a common survival technique and is accomplished in a variety of ways. Scientists speak of 'cryptic camouflage', meaning the use of shape and coloration to blend into the surroundings, a technique used by certain predators to conceal themselves as they lie motionless, patiently waiting for prey to venture close. Scorpionfish and stonefish are masters of this particular form of disguise. A feature of their technique is the lightning speed with which they can pounce when suitable prey comes within range.

Prey animals themselves are equally accomplished at the art of disguise, especially the juveniles of reef fishes. One very good example is the juvenile batfish. The shallows around mangroves are a favoured nursery area for these fishes, so the diminutive youngster mimics a dead mangrove leaf, matching its gold and brown coloration and floating near the surface, exactly like a curled leaf.

Some reef fishes are not always what they appear to be. The harmless leatherjacket, or false black-saddled pufferfish, for example, mimics the true pufferfish – one of the most poisonous fishes and immune from predators. Sometimes, such mimics so closely resemble the real thing that only experts can tell them apart. Behavioural camouflage is an even more subtle subterfuge to avoid detection. In this case, predatory reef fishes may hide within a shoal of harmless herbivorous fish, mimicking their coloration and swimming movements to approach and surprise their prey. The trumpetfish is one such behavioural camouflage expert and can imitate a number of non-carnivorous fish species.

Left: This tiny pufferfish looks harmless, but secretes a highly poisonous mucus over its body to deter predators. The harmless leatherjacket, in its turn, imitates the poisonous pufferfish to share its immunity from predation.

Above: Many reef fishes are vulnerable to their predators when young and mimic their surroundings in order to avoid becoming a meal. The juvenile batfish, for example, becomes a 'dead' mangrove leaf.

Left: The scorpionfish is a true master of the art of camouflage, mimicking most convincingly the encrusting growths that have surrounded the dead coral on this New Guinea reef.

Below: The Caribbean peacock flounder has the remarkable ability to change its coloration and body markings rapidly so it can match its surroundings.

Right: Predators are just as adept as their prey in the art of camouflaged concealment. The Atlantic trumpetfish, for example, hovers nose-down among the surrounding sea plumes, patiently waiting for a small fish or shrimp to pass close by. As soon as the unsuspecting prey approaches, the trumpetfish pounces and sucks it into its tubelike mouth.

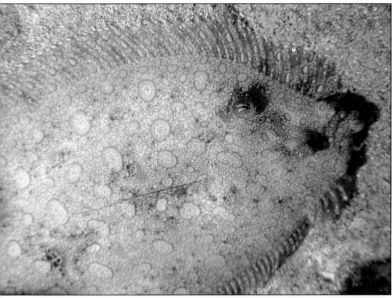

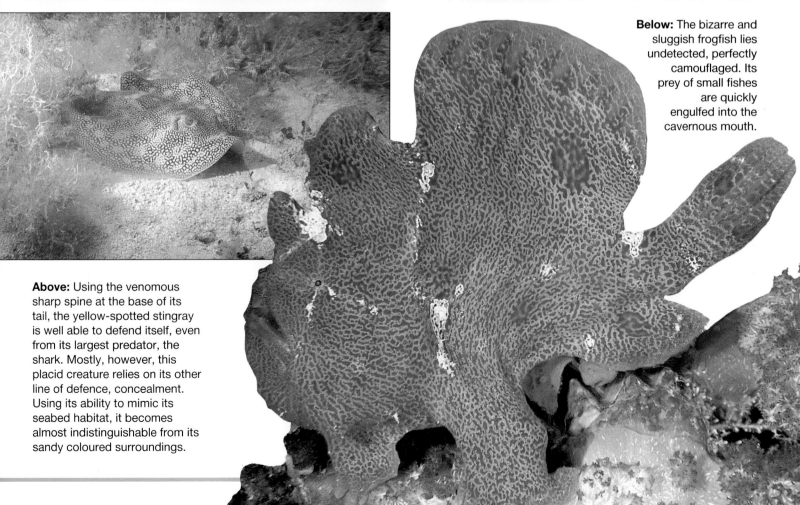

Below: The bizarre and sluggish frogfish lies undetected, perfectly camouflaged. Its prey of small fishes are quickly engulfed into the cavernous mouth.

Above: Using the venomous sharp spine at the base of its tail, the yellow-spotted stingray is well able to defend itself, even from its largest predator, the shark. Mostly, however, this placid creature relies on its other line of defence, concealment. Using its ability to mimic its seabed habitat, it becomes almost indistinguishable from its sandy coloured surroundings.

DON'T TOUCH!

Often, the most colourful animals on a coral reef are also the deadliest. Gaudy coloration is a clear warning of their defensive weapon, namely the ability to release poisonous mucus to evade predation. It is important that an animal using this method of defence is easily recognized by its predators before they decide to attack. Bright yellow combined with black spots or bars is the most universally popular form of warning coloration used both by terrestrial and aquatic animals. It is particularly effective in clear coral waters, where yellow is one of the few colours not filtered out by the blue of the ocean and is thus highly visible, even at considerable depths.

The juvenile form of the cube boxfish is a typical example of an animal that uses this technique to advertise its unpleasant-tasting mucus to keep it safe from attack. The vivid sea slugs share the same technique, using their brilliant colours to say 'look, but don't touch'. These delicate creatures - called nudibranchs because they display naked gills on their backs – are able to excrete highly distasteful toxic chemicals from glands in their skin.

Not all the 'don't touch' animals flaunt their presence so blatantly, especially those that rely on stings or sharp spines to deter predators. The coral reef can be an unpleasant place for the uninitiated – venomous fire corals, equally virulent stinging hydroids and spiny sea urchins abound in this crowded environment. One creature to avoid is the Indo-Pacific sea urchin *Asthenosoma varium*, which bristles with long, transparent, needle-shaped spines, each tipped with a poison sac, ready to deliver a painful wound as retribution for a casual touch.

Left: The exotic Spanish dancer is one of the largest and most colourful sea slugs. It is found in many parts of the Indo-Pacific and is common on the Great Barrier Reef of Australia. Its brilliant coloration advertises the unpleasant-tasting mucus secreted from glands on its skin.

Right: This Indo-Pacific sea slug sports the vivid coloration that warns it is not to be tampered with. Only an uninitiated predator would consider eating this gaudily coloured animal and would quickly withdraw on sampling the distasteful toxic chemicals secreted from its skir

Left: Coral reefs are places that should be approached with caution. Often, seemingly innocent creatures, such as this colourful *Asthenosoma* sea urchin, which bristles with long venomous transparent spines, can deliver painful wounds.

Right: This detailed look at a *Millepora* fire coral clearly shows the tiny stinging tentacles, or nematocysts as they are called, that discharge toxins into the skin. A casual brush against these tentacles is rewarded with a very painful burning sensation.

Left: Even the Antarctic has its 'look don't touch' animals. The colourful, many-tentacled Antarctic jellyfish could easily deliver a sting that could stun a person and cause a painful wound. Its tentacles are covered with tiny stinging cells.

Right: The Indo-Pacific lion- or turkeyfish is armed with highly venomous needle-sharp dorsal, anal and pelvic spines. Based on a neurotoxic venom very similar to that of the cobra, the sting can cause agonizing wounds that may prove fatal, but normally it is only used in self-defence.

Right: The perfect camouflage of the stonefish provides highly effective protection for the most venomous fish in the sea. Venom glands on either side of the dorsal spines are activated if stepped on. Often found in shallow tropical waters, the stonefish causes deaths each year.

PORCUPINEFISHES – ACE SURVIVAL EXPERTS

In devising means of protecting themselves from predators, reef life forms have a natural champion in the porcupinefishes. These aptly named fishes have the amazing ability to inflate themselves with water until they are much bigger than their normal size, presenting a large spiky ball to would-be predators. This remarkable strategy is only a first line of defence for the normally small, inoffensive porcupinefish, because it is also protected by a tough, horny skin. Furthermore, it is armed with teeth capable of crushing coral or delivering a nasty bite. And finally, its flesh contains a poison called tetraodontoxin.

As a result of this outstanding range of defences, porcupinefishes have remained effectively protected from their predators and are the most common fishes of the tropical oceans. Ironically, their ability to inflate themselves as a protection in the wild has resulted in their downfall at the hand of man. Inflated specimens are highly popular souvenirs, and many are collected each year for the curio trade to be dried, varnished and distributed around the world as ornaments. Due to this practice, porcupinefishes are close to becoming endangered in a number of areas. However, in one small way, porcupinefishes have exacted a revenge against their human enemy in parts of the world where these fishes are eaten as a delicacy. Each year, a number of deaths are recorded among people eating porcupinefish flesh contaminated with tetraodontoxin.

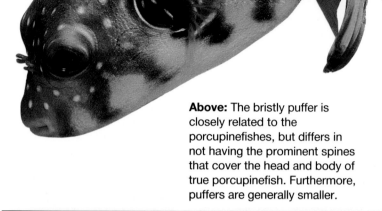

Above: The bristly puffer is closely related to the porcupinefishes, but differs in not having the prominent spines that cover the head and body of true porcupinefish. Furthermore, puffers are generally smaller.

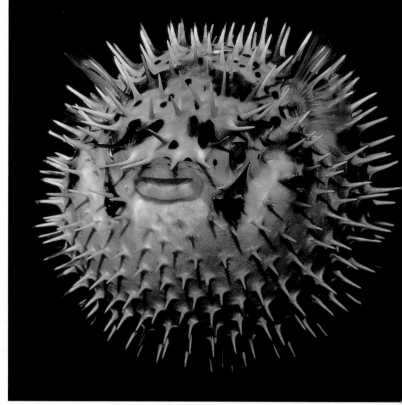

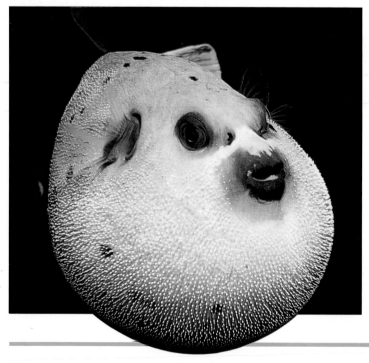

Left: The inflated clown puffer may not have the spines of its cousin, the porcupinefish, but it does have the same ability to inflate itself with water until it is many times its normal size, as is clearly shown here. All puffers also harbour a powerful toxin that can cause serious illness if the flesh of the fish is eaten.

Above: Fully inflated, the large balloonfish – a porcupinefish species distributed in the tropics worldwide – presents an impenetrable spiky ball to its predators. Few animals would, or could, attempt to swallow such an unpalatable meal and the porcupinefish is thus totally safe from predation in the wild.

The series of photographs on this page illustrate the amazing ability of the porcupinefish, here represented by the bridal burrfish, a small Caribbean porcupinefish species, to draw water into its body cavity and inflate to enormous proportions. Further armed by other defence mechanisms, including excellent camouflage in some cases, the porcupinefishes can truly be regarded as ace survival experts in the wild. Only man's appetite for curios threatens them.

Above: The spines of the burrfish are held erect, even when the fish is not inflated. In other species of porcupinefish, the spines are normally held close to the body and erected only when the fish inflates.

Right: Midway to full inflation, the burrfish changes in shape.

Below: The bridal burrfish, fully inflated and complete with spiky horns, is now incapable of normal swimming movement.

LIVING IN HARMONY

Any look at the teeming diversity of life on the coral reef would be incomplete without mentioning the many life forms that have learned to live together in harmony. Not all relationships on the coral reef are based on the aggressive predator versus prey, life or death struggle. Many interactions between animals - and also between animals and plants – are of a mutually beneficial nature and are described as symbiotic, which simply means 'living together'. In terms of the coral reef, the most important symbiotic relationship is the one between reef-building corals and the millions of single-celled plants – the microscopic zooxanthellae – that flourish within their tissues and 'capture' the energy of sunlight for the coral as well as for themselves.

There are many other forms of symbiosis between animals higher up the evolutionary scale. Cleaning symbiosis is a good example; a number of cleaner fish and cleaner shrimp species play a vital role in the reef community by cleaning parasites and pieces of dead tissue from other reef fishes. So popular is this practice that 'customers' are known to congregate at specific 'cleaning stations' on the reef.

Probably the best-known example of symbiosis in the fish world is that between the clownfish and its host anemone. Clownfish are a common feature of Indo-Pacific coral reefs, hovering above or weaving among the venomous tentacles of a large anemone. How the clownfish is able to enjoy immunity from the anemone's stinging tentacles, while other fishes are immediately stung, remained a mystery until relatively recently. It is now clear that the anemone's stinging

Above: There are many examples of harmonious relationships in the world of the coral reef. The best known is the fascinating relationship between the colourful clownfish and its very dissimilar partner, the anemone, a marine invertebrate.

response is triggered primarily by a chemical reaction, based on the anemone recognizing its prey by 'taste' on contact with the tentacles. The clownfish is able to disguise its natural body taste with a sugar-based mucus and also by gradually covering itself with mucus taken from the anemone. This fools the anemone's stinging mechanism and allows the clownfish to live within the protective tentacles, unmolested by the anemone and safe from other predators. In return, the brightly coloured clownfishes may act as a warning to deter would-be predators.

Left: The candy-striped cleaner shrimp stands sentinel at its cleaning station, waving its antennae to attract the attention of passing fish, so they can take advantage of its services.

Below: The cube boxfish is a regular customer for cleaning.

Above: The tiny porcelain crab nestles comfortably within the anemone's deadly stinging tentacles, knowing it is safe from predators. Like the clownfish, it is immune to the anemone.

Above: A common sight on the Great Barrier Reef of Australia is the large *Heteractis* anemone harbouring its attendant skunk clownfishes. These diminutive fishes are poor swimmers and rely entirely on the anemone for protection. Each anemone can play host to more than one fish.

Left: The symbiotic arrangement between the prawn goby and the pistol shrimp works perfectly. The shrimp provides a secure home and the goby repays it by using its keen eyesight to warn the shrimp of approaching danger.

Below: The Indo-Pacific cleaner wrasse also maintains a cleaning station, usually sited close to a prominent coral head, where fish arrive in swarms and wait patiently to be cleaned.

Right: There is obvious pleasure in the expression of this moray eel, tranquillized by the attentions of the cleaner wrasse. There is ample evidence to suggest that the tactile experience associated with the cleaning process is enjoyed by the cleaner's clients.

NIGHT AND DAY – AN ENDLESS CYCLE OF ACTIVITY

Certain terrestrial animals are active during the day, while others only wake up at night. The same can be said of marine animals; below the surface of the oceans, there is a constant cycle of activity throughout the day and night. In temperate and polar oceans, the nocturnal animals tend to be scavengers, mainly invertebrate forms. Spindly-legged crabs and lobsters scurry around in search of a dead animal or the remains of another animal's meal. Starfishes become very mobile, covering surprising distances in their nocturnal hunt for discarded remains. In tropical waters, competition for space and the availability of food have also forced some animals living on the coral reef to adapt to a nocturnal existence.

The 24-hour cycle on the coral reef begins at dawn, when the major predatory fish set out to hunt for breakfast. Large oceanic fish, such as jacks and pampano, coast the open ocean face of the reef, swooping down on their prey of small fish. As the sun rises, the reef is alive with a host of colourful reef fishes – tiny zooplankton-feeders, herbivores grazing on the strong growths of algae, and wily predatory groupers and other carnivores, ready to take advantage of any small fish sufficiently reckless to stray too close to their cavernous jaws. This colourful bustle continues into the late afternoon, when the daytimers retire to holes and crevices in the reef to make way for the night shift.

At night, the reef is a fascinating place, populated by strange animals that could be the product of a science-

fiction writer's imagination. Huge fan-shaped basket stars, relatives of the starfishes, spread their barbed arms to impale and capture the tiny crustaceans on which they feed. Their brilliantly coloured smaller cousins, the crinoid featherstars, climb high onto the reef and extend their arms to feed on small particles borne on the restless currents. Armies of black *Diadema* sea urchins with needle-sharp spines slowly advance from the depths to graze on algae in the shallows. Many stony and soft corals are also nocturnal feeders, feeding on the rich clouds of zooplankton that billow from the depths each night. And throughout the night, soldierfishes use their large eyes to pick up glimmers of light as they search for small fish and crustaceans.

Below and right: Reef fishes that are active during the day and rest at night often resort to night-time camouflage to evade predators. The daytime colours of the spotlight parrotfish shown right become muted at night (below).

Right: Spiny black *Diadema* urchins advance in silent hordes at night to feed on green algal pastures in the shallows.

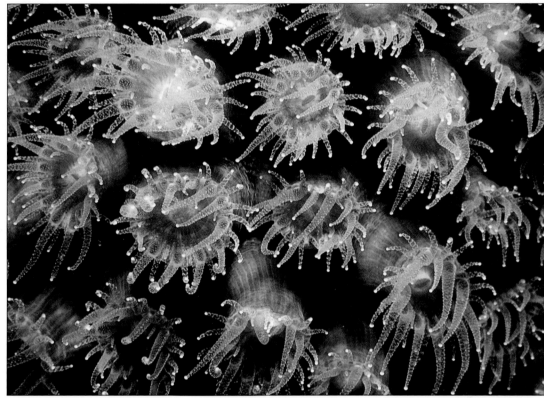

Above: Large eyes and red coloration distinguish nocturnal reef fishes from their daytime counterparts. The large eyes cope with low light levels and red coloration appears black.

Left: As darkness approaches, armies of nocturnal hunting soldierfishes pour out of their daytime lair to search for small fish and crustaceans. Their red coloration provides camouflage.

Right: The tiny polyps of reef corals extend to ensnare the zooplankton drifting by. The concentrations of plankton are at their highest at night, the time when many corals feed.

Below: The basket star has a matrix of tiny barbs covering its arms. It extends these arms to impale and capture the tiny crustaceans borne along on the passing water currents.

Above: Many crustaceans, such as this tiny hermit crab, are nocturnal scavengers, scurrying along the seabed in search of dead animals and scraps. In this way, they dispose of material that would only decompose and eventually pollute the water.

FILTER-FEEDERS – INEXORABLE AND EFFECTIVE CONSUMERS

Sea water is far denser than air and easily able to hold materials in suspension. Consequently, the waters of our oceans are not a sterile medium, but are filled with tiny suspended particles and contain all manner of dissolved chemicals. A number of life forms have taken advantage of what is really a nourishing 'soup' of both living and dead matter, and have evolved to become filter-feeders. They rely on their food coming to them, borne on water currents, and they spend their lives fixed to one spot – an unusual feature not generally found on land, where most animals are mobile. A close inspection of the seabed of any ocean reveals that large numbers of sessile (non-moving) animals have adopted this lifestyle with great success.

Fanworms are beautiful and delicate filter-feeders, with two feathery plumes held out in classic fan shapes. These fans use an efficient sievelike action to gather food and building materials for the tube-dwelling worm that bears them. The feathery appendages are located around the mouth and small particles trapped by them are passed by tiny hairlike cilia to a central food groove. Here they are sorted into three categories: large particles are discarded, medium-sized particles are taken as food and the small particles are mixed with mucus to build up the tube.

The fanworm's feeding technique is very successful, but it is not the only filtration device employed by marine life forms. Sponges, for example, filter vast

Above: The *Spirobranchus*, or Christmas tree worm, is a colourful example of a fanworm. Its sievelike feathery plumes collect and filter the suspended particles on which it feeds.

quantities of water to obtain food and oxygen, but in quite a different way. The sponge draws in water over its entire outer surface through tiny pores equipped with whiplike hairs. In the hollow centre of the sponge, the food and oxygen are absorbed and the water, plus any waste products, is expelled through a large central opening.

Left: The nocturnal crinoids are closely related to starfishes, but employ a similar filter-feeding technique to that of fanworms. They feed on zooplankton.

Below: The sponge has a maze of channels, each lined with tiny beating hairs that draw in water and food particles. The channels lead to a central chamber.

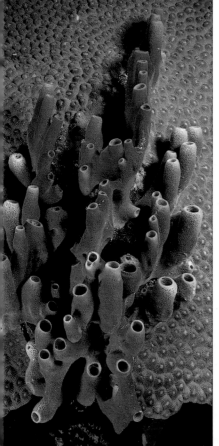

Left: Sponges are very diverse in form and most are shaped according to their environment. Their growth is dictated by the passing currents and their shape is designed to take the best advantage of these. Tubular sponges flourish in quiet waters.

Above: Not all filter-feeders are sedentary animals, waiting for their food to come to them. There are many mobile filter-feeders in the sea, including the manta ray, shown here, and the whale shark, as well as the mighty baleen whales.

Below: The sea cucumber uses yet a further variation on the filter-feeding technique. It has sticky feathery tentacles that trap the food particles, and each tentacle is placed in turn into the mouth, enabling the sea cucumber to swallow the food.

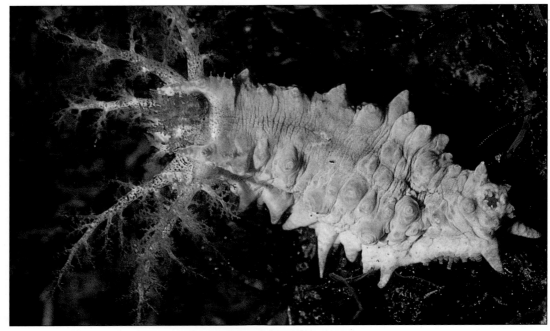

CARNIVORES OF THE OCEANS

Phytoplankton – microscopic drifting plants of the sea – are the basic food on which all ocean life ultimately depends. The next link in the food chain is filled by the zooplankton that feed on the phytoplankton, and they in turn become the main food supply for a wide range of carnivores – animals that feed on other animals – from tiny coral polyps to mighty filter-feeding whales.

Carnivorous animals that actively hunt for their prey are known as predators, and the open oceans are home to sleek, silvery hunters in the form of mackerel, tuna, jack, the ferocious barracuda and, of course, the oceanic sharks. All these creatures blend in perfectly with the sea and the silvery water surface, combining this camouflage with impressive speed to surprise their prey – usually small, shoaling zooplankton-feeding fish such as sardine and herring. Marine mammals use a similar technique; dolphins and seals have evolved a streamlined shape and are highly proficient swimmers. Torpedo-shaped squid and cuttlefishes are the sleek hunters among the invertebrates, their speed and well-developed eyes making them formidable predators.

In the remaining group of marine carnivores are those predators that rely on camouflaging themselves to look like features on the seabed. They can be further divided into 'lie-in-wait' hunters and those that stalk their prey. Masters of the lie-in-wait technique are flawlessly camouflaged and often adopt elaborate means of mimicking their surroundings. A large number of fish species fall into this category.

Anglerfish even provide a lure for small fish in the form of a fleshy appendage that twitches invitingly just above the cavernous mouth, while the Atlantic trumpetfish adopts a nose-down attitude and hovers in the water, realistically mimicking the swaying sea whips (see page 43). Of the fishes that stalk their prey, the grouper is perhaps the most expert, cleverly hiding its bulk with constantly changing camouflage and closing in imperceptibly on its prey.

Above: At the very top of the food chain, the barracuda is a sleek and effective predator, capable of achieving amazing bursts of speed in order to surprise and capture its chosen prey of small shoaling fishes.

Left: The flowerlike anemone may appear harmless, but even the heavily armoured crab is no match for the stinging tentacles and is quickly disabled and engulfed. The tentacles unfurl again quite rapidly after feeding.

Right: The squids are the next most important group of predators in the sea after the fishes. They are distributed in all the oceans and are found at all levels, from the surface layers down to the darkest depths.

Left: In the perpetual darkness of the abyss, predatory fishes often employ luminescent lures to attract their prey. They are further equipped with large mouths and needle-sharp teeth.

Right: The streamlined shape of the tuna and its large powerful tail allow this silvery predator to easily outswim its prey. Large quantities of fish such as sardines and herring are its principal diet.

Below: The Nassau grouper stalks its prey, blending easily into its surroundings.

Left: Flawless camouflage is a major part of the scorpionfish's hunting strategy. Any small fish or crustacean that happens to stray too close to the cavernous mouth is quickly overwhelmed. The spines are venomous.

Above: The open mouth of a bottlenose dolphin reveals the single row of peglike teeth along each jaw. These teeth are ideal for gripping the wide variety of fish, squid and octopi on which this and many dolphins feed.

SHARKS – SUPREME OCEAN PREDATORS

Sharks have ruled the oceans for 400 million years, primitive creatures so perfectly designed by nature that they have had no reason to evolve further. Although classified as a fish and a vertebrate, the shark is a very simple animal. It does not have gills like more 'modern' fish, only simple openings on either side of the head called pharyngeal slits, and its skeleton is made of cartilage or gristle, not bone. However, sharks do possess very sensitive and highly developed sensory organs. These are not based on sight and hearing – the main terrestrial senses – but largely on a remarkable sensitivity to vibration and taste.

The whole of a predatory shark's snout is covered with small pits. At the base of each pit are sensitive nerve endings capable of picking up vibrations over long distances and analyzing the form they take. This explains the speed with which a shark can arrive at the site of an injured fish; it accurately interprets the shock waves from the distressed victim thrashing in the water. Tests with the Pacific whitetip reef shark have revealed that animals can taste minute traces of blood in the water over long distances and home in on the source. Although the brain of the shark is fairly humble in an evolutionary sense, the sensory perception, swimming agility, sharp teeth and

ferocious disposition of the so-called man-eating sharks – among them the great white – combine to make these species formidable eating machines.

However, not all sharks share the fierce disposition of the great white and other streamlined hunters. The largest shark, the 12m(39.4ft)-long whale shark, is a perfectly harmless plankton-feeder that uses gill rakers, similar to a baleen whale's plates, to strain off plankton and small fishes. Another harmless species, the wobbegong, or carpet shark, is an unusual form, perfectly camouflaged to resemble a seaweed-covered rock. It is a lie-in-wait predator, ready to snap up any bottom-dwelling fish, mollusc or crustacean that ventures within reach of its jaws.

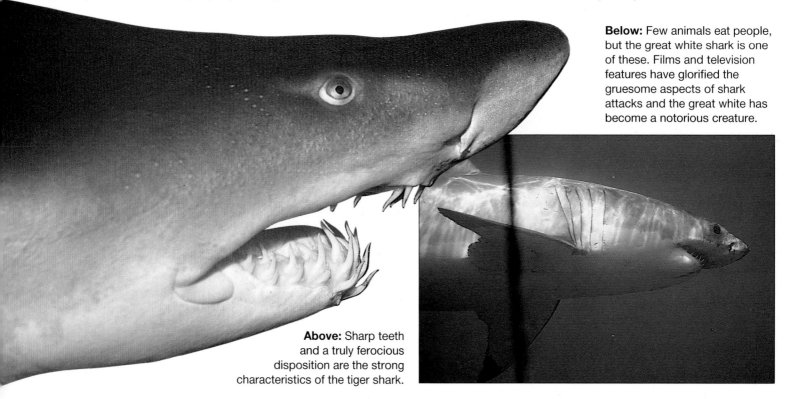

Below: Few animals eat people, but the great white shark is one of these. Films and television features have glorified the gruesome aspects of shark attacks and the great white has become a notorious creature.

Above: Sharp teeth and a truly ferocious disposition are the strong characteristics of the tiger shark.

Above left: The whitetip reef shark is not classed among the so-called man-eating sharks, and is a common visitor to the inshore reefs of the Indo-Pacific, where it can sometimes be seen in coral caves and lagoons.

Top: The Pacific provides a habitat for a large number of shark species, including the Pacific blacktip reef shark, which grows 1.5m(5ft) long.

Above: Of the ten or so main species of sharks that live in the Caribbean, the lemon shark is the most common. It may prove dangerous if provoked.

Right: Surprisingly, the highly camouflaged and harmless wobbegong is a member of the shark family. It lives among the weeds on shallow seabeds.

MAN RETURNS TO THE OCEAN

The world beneath the oceans has been described as 'inner space', the last frontier on earth. Technological advances now permit man to follow the example of the marine mammals and return to the ocean depths from where we first came. At present, we can only descend for brief periods, but the way is clear for us to obtain a first-hand and better understanding of the ocean world. This process is essential, because the oceans are the life force of the planet, producing the oxygen we breathe and, via evaporation, satisfying our fresh water requirements in the form of rain. The sun's energy provides a huge storehouse of phytoplankton that through the food web nourishes the fish and shellfish we catch for food. Properly farmed, the world's vast oceans are capable of producing a major proportion of our food on a truly sustainable basis.

Unfortunately, the more we learn about the sea, the more we appreciate the extent to which we have abused it in the past – and still do. Every day, vast amounts of rubbish and hazardous materials are tipped into the sea, all because it was once generally believed that the oceans were so huge that any pollution dumped there would be diluted and disappear. Now we find that dangerous substances are taken up in the food chain and concentrated until, eventually, they poison the seafoods we eat.

The extraction of the ocean's bounty has been no better managed; gross and wasteful overfishing not only severely depletes the stocks of animals we wish to catch, but also upsets the delicate balance of the ocean web of life. In ten years from now, it is conceivable that many of the life forms described in this book will no longer exist. Already, many existing whale species are at risk, as are certain species of seal and turtle, the dugong and penguins. Even sharks, the most tenacious survivors, are gradually being driven to extinction in some areas of the world; their slow breeding rate cannot keep pace with losses resulting from overfishing, particularly sport fishing along the western seaboard of the USA, and the huge numbers trapped in driftnets set in the Pacific Ocean.

Today, world attention is beginning to focus more sharply on environmental problems and the state of our oceans. We can only hope that by drawing attention to the abuse and overexploitation of the oceans we can persuade the nations of the world to avert the total destruction of our precious ocean life.

Above: The exploration of the world's oceans will help us to discover the secrets of inner space. Armed with this greater understanding, we should also be able to find better ways of conserving the ocean world.

Left: Most of the sea fisheries of the world have been grossly overexploited. The answer to this problem must be to farm the oceans on a sustainable basis and avoid overfishing.

Right: Crude oil spillage has become one of the most common forms of sea pollution over the past decade. The consequences of such spillage are devastating to marine life.

Left: Fish farming can take many forms and can be very successful. Here, Atlantic salmon are being reared in floating pens off Ediz Hook near Port Angeles, Washington.

Above: A kelp harvester off the Californian coast uses modern sustainable methods of harvesting the rich fields of kelp. The harvester will return to find a new crop the following year.

Above: One method of saving an endangered species from extinction is the use of mariculture. Here, baby green sea turtles are reared in captivity for release directly into the sea, avoiding the risk of predation.

Below: Most forms of sea life are seriously affected by the consequences of oil pollution. Such pollution is a major threat to all the oceans of the world and every year many millions of marine animals are killed.

INDEX

Page numbers in **bold** indicate major references, including accompanying photographs. Page numbers in *italics* indicate captions to other illustrations. Less important text entries are shown in normal type.

PICTURE CREDITS